Thoughts I Don't Express

Heather Simpson

Presentation by *BookLeaf Publishing*

Web: www.bookleafpub.com

E-mail: info@bookleafpub.com

ISBN: 9789357743785

First edition 2023

Enough?

Abuse, hatred, and longing for any kind of love
My childhood wasn't filled with that.

Nightmares that became reality
My childhood wasn't filled with that.

Betrayal and likes from trusted adults
My childhood wasn't filled with that.

Confusion and upset from familiar peers
My childhood had a little of that.

Rumors, gossip, and backstabbing from friends
My childhood had a little of that.

Liked but not loved
My childhood had a little of that.

A twinge of trauma, a pang of pain
Is it enough to validate who I am?

Dungeons and Dragons

Fantastical lands
Mythological creatures
Magical, beautiful beings
Light fights against the dark
Heroes and villains clash in epic conflict
Everything anyone ever wanted to be
But looked down upon so many

Fear

Patiently, silently waiting in the shadows
Under your bed
Hiding in your closet
The monster that grabs your feet in the night
Green eyes
No, red eyes, glowing in the dark
Lurking
Ever present
Ready to strike when the moment is right
No escape
How do you fight?
It's all in your mind

Cousin (June 27 1985- July 4th 2008)

Through the good times and the bad
The many moves and broken hearts
Not knowing what will happen next
And falling into despair
A young boy grown into a young man
Not knowing who to turn to
Only because you never had that one shoulder
to cry on
Long for a little acceptance from the ones you
love
Turning to the wrong crowd
You felt accepted and wanted
Pushing your family aside
Only because of the love you didn't feel from
one
It is time to realize
You are in danger if you stay on this path
Trust the ones who have always shown you
what you need
For we are the ones who will always be with
you in your heart

18

A girl was born into this world
One who was small, quiet, and had a turtle head

For eighteen years she grew and matured
Yet for the most part she stayed the same

Fun, caring, and bright
As some people would describe her

Her soul seems to be magic
She just knows how to cheer someone up

She is always around when you need her
Even if she isn't around, she's always there

Some say she's mean and rude
But she doesn't let that get to her

She refuses to change just because someone
dislikes her
"If they don't like me then that's fine with me."

She's full of morals
That most teenagers don't have

She knows that she's odd for her age
But that's what makes her special in her own
little way

If there were more like her around
The world be so mean

If I were this girl, which I am
I wouldn't change a thing about me

One Friend

I'll tell you a story
  A lonely girl found a friend
 Who seemed to fall from thin air
 They talked everyday about things that didn't
matter
 Of dogs and cats to love and life
 As the days slowly past, hour after hour
 They slowly began to know one another
 Time passes and finally a year goes by
 Not even a squall between the two
 The girl decides to show her thanks
 So thank you my friend for bringing me out of
my hole
 For turning my world into someone grand
 Thank you for the shoulder you let me cry on
 And for the times you made me laugh
 But most of all thank you for the love you've
shown me
 Without, my world would be dead

Miss you

Seconds tick by
 The shock slowly fades

Minutes tick by
The tears trickle down my cheeks

Hours tick by
I feel like I can't breathe

Days tick by
Grief washes over me

Weeks tick by
What is the point of it all?

Months tick by
The pain fades, but it never goes away

A year ticks by
I can't remember a time in which I don't miss
you

How did I turn into this?

Frustration fueled by promises of change
Annoyances inflamed by condescension
When did you start to think you were better
than me?
Dislike provoked by mansplaining
Resentment induced by not listening
You hate that other people do it, but you do it
too?
Questions stimulated by gaslighting
But maybe not?
Not trusting myself influenced by a lack of
understanding
Can I fix what has been done
Or do I deserve this somehow?

Single

Strong and independent to a fault
I'm not sure why it happened
Communication is a weakness
I don't like confrontation or vulnerability
Fear chokes me to the point of indecisiveness
I'm terrified of acceptance and rejection
Quiet, shy, and cautious are dominant traits
Am I worth the effort?
Guilt or maybe shame is a constraint
Apparently, it's wrong to like men younger than me
Age is slowly creeping along
I might be alone forever

Why?

I want to quit my job.
 Why?
 I want to travel.
 Why?
 I feel like I'm stuck.
 Why?
 I feel jaded inside
 Why?
 I'm lacking challenge and inspiration
 Why?
 I'm just going through the motions.
 Why?
 I need meaningful change.
 Why?

Photography

Something I love
 A hobby at best
Started on a whim
I was good, but I wasn't the best

"The eye" was there
Talent needed refinement
Developed new abilities
All on my own

The joy I feel
Being in my element
Not many understand
But I don't care

Change

Virulent environment
Saturates my core
Fatigued mind
Yearning for something more
Taxing six years
Trying to open another door
Practically there
My chance to explore
Meaningful shift
I can't ignore

Maybe I'm...

Maybe I'm selfish
I desire a deeper connection
But maybe I'm shallow
I want a handsome face for my affection
Maybe I'm scared
There is always rejection
But maybe I'm hopeful
His love could be perfection
Maybe I'm clingy
I can't handle more neglection
But maybe I'm smart
Please don't used your intellect for misdirection
Maybe I'm suspicious
Help me work on communication
But maybe I try
Understanding is needed for this correction

Breadcrumbs

Subtle glances, teasing smiles
 That was all that it was
 Then you interlocked your fingers with mine
 Why?
 I told you I liked you
 Against better judgement
 Expecting rejection
 But you pressed me for more
 You couldn't be mine, so why?
 Soft touches, enchanting words
 You sprinkled me with desire
 And I provided you with what you craved
 Why tease me with breadcrumbs
 If you had no intention to stay?

Don't call me

Don't call me honey
I'm not your honey

Don't call me baby
Oh how I hate to be called baby

Don't call me sweetheart
It's condescending to be called sweetheart

Don't call me queen
It's not empowering to be a queen

Don't call me goddess
Unless I'm a fairy moon goddess

Don't call me sugar
Even if I can be sweet like sugar

Don't call me darling
I don't want to be your darling

Rain

Gradually descending
Lazily sprinkling the outside
A flash of lightning, a rumble of thunder
Enough to scare living beings to shelter

Intensely cascading
Drenching the empty pavement
As night enshrouds the land
Free to swirl upon a barren environment

Seemingly cleansing
Free reign over a dark spring night
Haltingly lessens
As the dawn approaches

Lost

Surrounded by light
But a gentle chill touches your skin
Supposedly happy, enveloped by love
But the spiraling turmoil is creeping in
Wearily displaying confidence
But the fatigue is draining
Stupidly smiling
But the silent screams for help are deafening
Bathed in light
But you can't escape the sun

Grief

The shock echoes down to your toes
 Momentary tears trickle down your cheeks
 Numbness cushions the blow
 Pretending to be fine to protect your mind

 An unexplainable rage burns
 Bursts of hot tears evaporate from the fire
within
 Passionate hate towards everything especially
the departed
 You left this world too soon

 Intolerable agony shreds your insides
 Imploring anyone who will listen
 You'll do anything for the misery to subside
 While guilt strangles the soul

 Hopelessness settles in
 Your eyes hurt from the onslaught of tears
 Sometimes it's hard to breathe
 As the sorrow drags you under

 Reality is bleak
 But the tears are diminishing
 The cycle is constant
 But now is a new beginning

www.ingramcontent.com/pod-product-compliance
Lightning Source LLC
LaVergne TN
LVHW050851200726
843508LV00013B/3038